25 BIRDS

One Year · One Garden

Anna K. Wood

25 Birds. One Year · One Garden

Published by Anna K. Wood 2022
Photographs and Text © Anna K. Wood 2022

ISBN 9781739139100

FOREWORD

I have enjoyed watching birds for a number of years, but it was only in October 2020, inspired by Carl Bovis on Twitter (@CarlBovisNature), that I started trying to photograph them – initially with varying degrees of success! Photographing birds gives me so much joy because it forces me to pay attention to them: their behaviour, their interactions with other birds, the way they fly, their song, and how all these change over the course of the year.

I know that I am lucky to have a small garden in which to watch birds, and I have especially appreciated this since becoming housebound with severe Myalgic Encephalomyelitis (ME, a chronic illness in which the body does not produce energy properly). 'Housebound' is a difficult concept to describe as it means different things to different people. For me it means that 95% of the time I'm either too unwell to leave the house, or the payback from doing so (technical term: PEM – Post Exertional Malaise) would cause me an unacceptable level of suffering.

Having ME means that the choice of photographic equipment is crucial. All the photos in this book were taken with a Sony Alpha a6000 together with a Sony E-mount 70-350mm lens. The Sony Alpha is a mirrorless camera which is much lighter than a standard DSLR. The weight is really important because the muscles in my arms tire easily and shaking arms do not lead to good pictures!

I hope that reading this book will give you just as much joy as I have had from watching and photographing birds over the last year.

HOUSE SPARROW

House sparrows are one of the most frequent birds to visit my garden, yet until I started photographing them I did not appreciate their beauty. In some areas there has been a significant decline in sparrow populations in recent years, but numbers are now recovering. I love this photo of a male sparrow with a pigeon feather, collected to help line the nest. I was really lucky that the light was just right to capture the detail of both the plumage and the feather in its beak. Watching them trying to chase and pick them up was very amusing, and clearly not an easy thing for them to do. However, as this was a common sight in spring, the feathers were obviously much sought after.

MAGPIE

I can't say that magpies are my favourite birds, but they are extremely clever. They can make and use tools, and can even recognise themselves in a mirror! Magpies can also work together to achieve a goal: when scientists attempted to study the birds by attaching trackers to them, they collaborated to remover the trackers from each other. Magpies are members of the corvid family, which also includes crows, jackdaws, and jays. There is even a corvid research unit in Cambridge, which was saved in 2022 from closure after a huge fundraising campaign.

It took a lot of attempts to take a good photo of a magpie, particularly because they are very shy when humans are around, but also because the contrast of the white and the black of their feathers makes it tricky to get an exposure that shows details in the dark areas without washing out the features in the lighter areas. I took this photo when a neighbour parked his red van to the side of the house. The van gives a dramatic backdrop to the photo and contrasts with the black and white of the bird's feathers.

STARLING

Starlings are beautiful birds with iridescent feathers that look stunning when they catch the light. Sadly they are on the UK Red List, which means that they are in critical decline. This might seem odd as when we think of starlings we also think of murmurations – the wonderful displays of often thousands of birds flying in a coordinated group, swirling and twirling together. But these numbers are bolstered by starlings from Eastern Europe that come to the UK for the winter. Given their declining numbers, it was particularly wonderful to have small groups of starlings nesting nearby this year. One pair almost nested in a hole in my neighbour's wall. For a few weeks I watched them flying back and forth, bringing twigs in, but in the end they didn't stay. I did, however, see juvenile starlings a few weeks later, so at least some local starlings must have bred successfully.

GREENFINCH

Although I've seen greenfinches in local green spaces on the rare occasions that I've been able to get out, 2022 was the first time in around 16 years that they have come into the garden. This photo is of a male. As is common in birds, the male is more brightly coloured than the female. I thought their appearance was probably a one-off, that they had been brought in by bad weather and the lure of an easy meal, but both the male and the female have become semi-regular visitors. They do tend to come when it is cloudy and rainy though, so getting a photo was very tricky! They can also be very hard to tell apart from the sparrows in poor light even with their green stripe. Eventually I noticed that greenfinches behave differently – they tend to sit in one position at the seed feeder for much longer than sparrows. I still have to pay very close attention to distinguish them.

HERRING GULL

It can seem strange that most cities in the UK, even those a long way from the sea, have what we often call 'seagulls'. The word doesn't cover a single species of bird, but instead is a term we use for a variety of gulls, including herring gulls and common gulls. Both these species have adapted to an urban life, but common gulls are not actually that common, so if you see a gull inland it is more likely to be a herring gull. One way to tell them apart is that herring gulls sport a red spot on their beak, while common gulls do not. Unfortunately, herring gulls are on the UK Red List, due to the decline in their marine populations, although those in our cities are thriving.

GOLDFINCH

Goldfinches are my favourite birds. The vibrant colours of yellow in the wing and red on the head seem so out of place for a British bird, yet they are frequent visitors to our gardens all through the year. The collective name for a flock of goldfinches is a charm, which is certainly a fitting term for such delicate creatures. I once saw a charm of goldfinches that must have consisted of over 100 birds. The sight was amazing, but it is the noise that I remember most; their chattering song is complex and easily recognisable. I often hear them flying overhead but on occasion they come into the garden to feed on dandelion heads or other flowers which have been left to go to seed in our unmown lawn. You can attract them to your garden with nyjer seed, but I prefer to watch them hopping, hovering, and fluttering in the long grass.

BLUE TIT

While luck always plays a role in bird photography, shots like this one also require persistence and patience. I was in the back garden when I heard a small group of blue tits arrive. I tracked them down to a neighbour's tree which hangs over my drive – perfect for photography. Amongst the group were some juvenile blue tits which were sitting on a branch waiting for the adult to bring them food. Again, perfect for photography. However, it takes less than a second for the adult to arrive, give the juvenile food and leave again, so getting a good shot was not easy. It took a lot of standing and waiting for the perfect moment, holding the camera in place until the adult returned. I was exhausted by the end, but I got a photo that I'm really proud of.

JUVENILE HOUSE SPARROW

Watching young birds is always a delight. This juvenile house sparrow was being fed by an adult male sparrow just coming into shot on the right. It spent a lot of time with its beak wide open and making increasingly insistent calls. Fledgling birds also flutter their wings and shake as a way of indicating they want food. Most of the time this one was hidden further back in the tree, but for a while it was visible enough on this branch that I could get a photo. One bonus of photographing birds when the young are being fed is that both they and their parents are so busy that they are a bit less bothered about humans, so it's possible to get closer than normal.

GREAT SPOTTED WOODPECKER

It has been such a joy to have regular visits from woodpeckers during the spring and summer of 2022. This is a male (it has a red stripe on its neck which isn't visible in the photo), but I've also seen the female (which has no red markings on the neck). At first, it was common for them to feed from the fat balls we put out for them, then fly off to a nearby tree, slowly moving up the trunk collecting insects. After a couple of weeks their behaviour changed; they started coming more regularly, filling their beaks with chunks of the fat balls before flying off in the direction of the park, to return a few minutes later for more. One evening they came at least seven times. I guessed (and hoped) that they were feeding young, and it turns out they were (see the photos of the juvenile great spotted woodpecker later in this book). I must have spent a fortune on fat balls but it was worth it!

JUVENILE STARLING

One of the wonderful things about birdwatching is noticing how the birdlife changes with the seasons. For a few weeks in late spring the garden was mobbed by juvenile starlings. It was wonderful to see that they had bred successfully, but they made so much noise I was worried they would disturb the neighbours! Juvenile starlings have fluffy brown-grey plumage, which helps protect them from predators. Then, like this young bird in the photo, they start to develop the darker-patterned feathers of an adult. This change starts with the body feathers and ends with the head, but often there are patches of brown while this is happening, which could be confusing when identifying them.

LONG–TAILED TIT

Long–tailed tits are another of my favourite birds. They have tiny bodies with shades of grey, hues of pink, and a very long tail (hence the name). They are normally seen in gardens in the winter, when they arrive in loud tweeting flocks to feed. Then in the spring they disappear to local woods to breed. This year, however, they returned with their new families in August. At one point I counted ten in the plum tree!

Long-tailed tits mate for life and form a strong bond. When all the others had disappeared this spring one pair kept coming to feed on the fat balls. It was easy to tell it was the same pair as one of them had lost its tail, possibly to a cat or a sparrowhawk. I nicknamed it the no-tailed tit and was pleased to see that the loss of its tail didn't seem to hinder the bird at all. A few weeks later I was thrilled to observe the tail was growing back.

JUVENILE DUNNOCK

Luck plays such a huge part in bird photography and this is especially true for me, as I can't get out to go and find birds; instead, I have to wait and hope they come to me. On the day I took this picture I was lying in the hammock in the garden when something small and fluffy flew into the clematis bush behind me. I immediately went to get my camera, expecting the bird to have flown off by the time I got back, but surprisingly it was still around and was very happy to pose near me while I took some photographs. I was delighted when I realised it was a juvenile dunnock as this was the first time I had seen one.

COAL TIT

This is one of those photos which combines luck with planning. Our next-door neighbour has a cherry tree with the most beautiful white blossoms. I'd noticed it the previous year but hadn't managed to get any good shots of birds in it, so I was determined to try again this year. Eventually the blossom came out, but then the weather was either too cloudy, too wet, or too windy. Of course, on the rare occasions that it was sunny I was too unwell to be outside taking photos! Eventually everything came together, and I was up early enough to catch both the sun and the birds. I hid behind a wheely bin, using it as support as I can't stand for very long. I was really aiming for blue tits, but this coal tit came along at just the right time, and I was really pleased with the result.

Song Thrush, Juvenile Goldfinch, Bullfinch, Tree Sparrow

Song Thrush (top left). I get visits from various members of the thrush family; fieldfares, mistle thrushes, and song thrushes. Like this song thrush, they are attracted by the red berries near my garden.

Juvenile Goldfinch (top right). Juvenile goldfinches have the tell-tale yellow wing feathers, but not the red on the head which marks the adult. This was my first photo of a juvenile goldfinch and I took it while sitting outside getting some sun before breakfast one bright spring day. Luckily I had my camera to hand as it didn't stay long!

Bullfinch (bottom left). Bullfinches are quite rare in my garden, so it is always an exciting event when they appear. This is a male, and, as is common in birds, he is much more brightly coloured than the female.

Tree Sparrow (bottom right). Tree sparrows and house sparrows look very similar, but although they are members of the same family, they are in fact two different species. Tree sparrows have a completely brown head, whereas house sparrows have a brown stripe on either side of a grey band down the centre of the head. Tree sparrows are much rarer than house sparrows so I wasn't expecting to see one in my garden. I didn't even realise that I had taken a photo of a tree sparrow until later in the day when I was looking through the camera roll.

JUVENILE GREENFINCH

Greenfinches used to be common garden birds, but in 2006 numbers were decimated by a fungal infection. While I have seen the adults many times, I hadn't ever seen a juvenile greenfinch until this year – and then three came all at once! It is wonderful to know that they are breeding successfully. They are unmistakably greenfinches, with a yellow-green stripe on their tail feathers, pale green upperparts and a finch's beak, but unlike the adults, the juveniles have a speckled belly.

ROBINS

The robin has been voted Britain's most bird popular bird, and it's easy to see why. Their red breast and funny bobbing motion always make me smile. They are particularly visible during the winter, brightening up even the dullest of days. Robins are often very happy to be near humans, and I've heard about people even managing to feed them out of their hand! One would think, then, that they'd be easy to photograph, but for some reason this is not the case for our local robins, which insist on singing high up in a tree, or in a bush mostly out of sight. It took me weeks of trying before I got these shots! I'm particularly pleased with the photo of the two robins together as they are mostly solitary creatures, only coming together to mate and raise their chicks. This photo shows one robin bringing an offering of a grub to its potential partner.

JUVENILE WOODPECKER

It seemed likely that the woodpeckers visiting us were feeding young, but I didn't expect I would actually see their nest. I am not often well enough to undertake the 10-minute mobility scooter ride to the local park, but one day I felt I could manage it, so decided to have a look. It turned out the nest was easy to find – the call of the hungry juvenile gave away its location just off the main path. I managed a few quick photos but was careful not to disturb it. A couple of weeks later the male brought the juvenile (with the distinctive red head) to visit and I watched him feeding peanuts and chunks of fat balls to the young one, who was sat in a tree nearby. Great spotted woodpeckers split parenting very equitably with each taking responsibility for some of the brood, though in this case it seems there was only one chick.

GREAT TIT

Great tits are the most common bird in my garden and they love the peanuts and the sunflower seeds I put out, but I have not been very successful at getting a good photograph of them. Partly this is because they move so quickly, flitting from branch to branch, but also because they are much shyer than other birds. I often sit outside, partially hidden, but close enough to the feeders to take photos. The blue tits and coal tits don't mind too much but the great tits are much more wary. They generally stay away, and if they do come close they quickly grab seeds then hide in the tree. This one landed on a fence nearby and I was delighted to get the photo before it flew off.

FERAL PIGEON

I love taking close-ups of birds, especially when I can get a photo at eye level as it gives a special intimacy to the shot. For this photo I sat on the drive of my house, as I do for many photos, because I can't stand up for very long. This usually means I have to look right up into a tree to get a photo, but when a pigeon wandered nearby I realised that for once I was at just the right level. I had no idea that feral pigeons were so beautiful. I particularly like the iridescent green neck. I still find it annoying that they trample all over the flowerbeds beneath the bird feeders, picking up the crumbs dropped by other birds, but I have a newfound admiration for them – after all, they are birds too.

JACKDAWS

Jackdaws, like magpies, are another bird that is easily dismissed as uninteresting. When they descend on the feeders and eat through an entire week's supply of fat balls in just a few minutes it can feel very frustrating and I have a strong temptation to chase them off to allow the smaller birds to feed. But they really are quite magnificent birds. I was delighted to capture this adult feeding a juvenile, though it does look as if it has put the food right down the young one's throat! The juvenile is amazingly only slightly smaller than the adult (probably because of all the fat balls it has eaten) but is fluffier and doesn't yet have the distinct grey neck. It is great fun watching them learn how to get their own food from the feeders.

CHIFFCHAFF AND WILLOW WARBLER

Over the last couple of years, I noticed that at the height of summer, for just a few weeks, these small yellow birds visited the garden. I thought they were willow warblers, but I then learned that they could have been chiffchaffs, which look very similar. This year however, I have definitely had both chiffchaffs (top picture) and willow warblers (bottom picture) in the garden. They are extremely difficult to tell apart unless they are singing, which of course they aren't at the time of year I see them. Some experts on Twitter and in the Scottish Ornithologists' Club very kindly helped me with identification. One key difference is the leg colour and another is the length of the stripe around the eye. They also make calls that are very similar but not quite identical – I'm still working on learning how to tell them apart!

DUNNOCK

I love photographing dunnocks. They are such under-appreciated birds, but they have beautiful markings. I only learned to tell the difference between dunnocks and sparrows quite recently. Although dunnocks used to be called hedge sparrows, they aren't actually sparrows at all, but from the family of accentors. The quickest way to tell the difference between a sparrow and a dunnock is to look at the beak. A dunnock beak is thin and pointy, whereas a sparrow has a much fatter finch-like beak. Dunnocks tend to sit still for a little longer than many other birds which makes photographing them slightly easier. I took this photo when the bird came to land on the fence just outside my lounge window, which made it possible to get a really close shot without spooking it.

WOOD PIGEON

One of the things I love about taking photos of birds is seeing the detail that I would otherwise miss. I had no idea that wood pigeons had so many features: the orange beak, the strips of green and white on the neck, the bright yellow eyes. Pigeons are very common in gardens and parks, where they are often thought of as a nuisance, so it's easy to see them, but not really notice them. I love trying to appreciate the details of all birds and photographing them strongly encourages me to do that.

JUVENILE BLUE TIT

During the 2020 COVID-19 lockdown I started using an app called BirdNet which records birdsong and gives you its best guess of which birds are nearby. It's not perfect, but it has encouraged me to listen more closely to birds and to learn some of the songs that I commonly hear in the garden. Paying close attention to bird song has helped my photography, because now I'm always listening out to hear what birds are around and as soon as I hear something different I try to see what it is and whether it is close enough to photograph. Listening is what alerted me to the arrival of these beautiful young blue tits. They were so small and fluffy I couldn't stop taking photographs of them! The young birds have yellow heads, which can be confusing given their name. The blue typically seen in adults develops a few weeks later.

FEMALE HOUSE SPARROW

Female house sparrows are perhaps the most nondescript bird I see in the garden. They seem to be mostly brown, but when you look closely you see that they have a lovely mix of deep brown, light brown, and even white on the wing feathers, with soft brown underneath. During the breeding season they lay between two and five eggs at daily intervals. Once they have hatched, the young birds rely on their parents for food for the first week of their life (see the picture of a juvenile sparrow earlier in the book).

ACKNOWLEDGEMENTS

Thank you to everyone who has played a part in bringing this book to life, especially to Kristin Houlihan and Phil Mason for editorial guidance. Thank you also to Tanya Marlow for proof reading and Abigail Simmonds for sharing her design expertise. Particular thanks to Ellie Conway and Germaine Hypher for being a sounding board for all my ideas and for always making sensible suggestions, and to Sally Doherty for such helpful advice about self-publishing. Of course, a huge thank-you to all my friends on Facebook and Twitter for enjoying, commenting on, and sharing my photos, and for encouraging this project in the first place. I am grateful to the Scottish Ornithologists' Club, Clyde Branch, for advice about bird identification, and also to Bruce Taylor and other experts on Twitter. Finally, thank you to my wonderful husband Phil for being so supportive of my endeavours, and for agreeing to us buying an expensive camera!

Printed in the USA
CPSIA information can be obtained
at www.ICGtesting.com
LVHW071916011123
762817LV00009B/35